ladieslovetodish

Bite-sized beginnings sure to have everyone talking.

let's talk apps.

Wrapped.

Rolled. Skewered. And stuffed.

We've served it all up with 26 mouthwatering

appetizer recipes. From dips and spreads to pancakes

and pâtés, it's a collection of finger foods made terrifically

more fabulous. So gather your friends and get ready to dish.

Because these apps have just the touch of attitude

that will not only have everyone talking

but might just leave them

speechless.

table *of* contents

recipes

surf and turf asparagus 6

asian wonton cups 8

lamb chops with two sauces 12

note: food terms 15

orange-scented carrot soup 18

poblano chili soup 18

roasted red pepper soup 19

dilled beet soup 19

festive feta and avocado salsa 20

wasabi reds 22

sweet on swedish pancakes 26

herbed goat cheese balls 28

from focaccia with love 32

savory smoked salmon cheesecake 34

note: food garnishing ideas 37

spinach pesto 38

shrimp-a-go-go 40

note: glassware decorating tips 42

mesquite chicken and toasted pecan pâté 46

roasted grape and mascarpone bruschetta 48

note: invite and decor tips 51

sweet honey blues 54

note: the perfect cheese tray 57

red pepper relish 58

garlic shrimp with cheddar grits 60

cranberry-pistachio brie 62

scallop bundles with orange-tarragon butter 66

petite pork tenderloin burgers 70

chicken gouda pumpernickel squares 70

mini gyros burgers with feta aioli 71

note: facts on herbs 73

parmesan lace 74

note: creativity with candles 76

surf and turf asparagus

Recipe inspired by Bernice Novello

Crisp asparagus spears look gorgeous wrapped in velvety, rich lox and paper-thin prosciutto.

1 package (3 ounces) cream cheese, room temperature

2 ounces nova lox or fresh smoked salmon, finely chopped

1 tablespoon finely chopped chives or green onion

8 thin slices prosciutto, cut in half

16 medium or 32 thin asparagus spears, blanched

16 long chives

Cantaloupe slices

Mix cream cheese, lox and chives; spread on one side of prosciutto halves. Wrap a prosciutto half around 1 medium or 2 thin asparagus spears and tie with a chive. Repeat with remaining asparagus, prosciutto and chives. Arrange on platter and serve with cantaloupe slices. *Makes 8 servings.*

asian wonton cups

Spicy wasabi peas give these crunchy cups filled with brightly colored veggies some added kick.

24 wonton wrappers
Sesame oil
1 cup sliced napa cabbage
½ cup thinly sliced snow peas
½ cup shredded carrots
½ cup clover or broccoli sprouts
1 green onion and top, thinly sliced
Sesame Dressing (recipe follows)
Wasabi peas, as garnish

Lightly brush edges of wonton wrapper with sesame oil. Press wonton, oil side up, into mini-muffin cup to form pastry shell. Repeat with remaining wonton wrappers, pressing into every other cup in muffin tin so that edges do not touch. Bake at 350 degrees until lightly browned, 6 to 7 minutes. Cool on wire racks. Combine cabbage, snow peas, carrots, broccoli sprouts and green onion in bowl; pour Sesame Dressing over and toss. Spoon about 1 tablespoon mixture into each wonton cup; garnish each with 2 or 3 wasabi peas. *Makes 8 servings (2 each).*

sesame dressing

3 tablespoons canola oil
1 tablespoon sesame oil
3 tablespoons rice wine vinegar
¼ cup apricot preserves
1 teaspoon soy sauce
1 teaspoon minced gingerroot
2-3 teaspoons peanut butter

Mix all ingredients until combined. *Makes about ½ cup.*

"

Hors d' OEUVRES

IS *simply* FRENCH

FOR

'let's PARTY.'

"

lamb chops with two sauces

Perfectly seared lamb chops are made irresistible with easy minted marmalade and peppered-rosemary dipping companions.

16 frenched rib lamb chops (1½ - 2 ounces each)
Salt and pepper, to taste
Minted Marmalade Sauce (recipe follows)
Peppered-Rosemary Mustard Sauce (recipe follows)
Small lettuce leaves and baby squash halves

Broil lamb chops 6 inches from heat source to desired degree of doneness, about 2 minutes on each side for medium; sprinkle lightly with salt and pepper. Spoon Minted Marmalade and Peppered-Rosemary Mustard Sauces into lettuce leaves and baby squash halves or into small bowls; arrange on serving platter with lamb chops. *Makes 8 servings.*

minted marmalade sauce

¼ cup finely chopped onion
1 clove garlic, minced
Generous pinch red pepper flakes
1 tablespoon olive oil
½ cup packed light brown sugar
¼ cup water
¼ cup orange marmalade
2 tablespoons finely chopped fresh mint leaves

Sauté onion, garlic and red pepper flakes in oil in small skillet until tender, 2 to 3 minutes. Stir in brown sugar and water; cook over medium heat until brown sugar is dissolved. Add orange marmalade and bring to boil; reduce heat and simmer, uncovered, until slightly thickened, about 3 minutes. Stir in mint. Serve warm or at room temperature. *Makes about ⅔ cup.*

peppered-rosemary mustard sauce

3 tablespoons Dijon mustard
2 tablespoons sugar
2 tablespoons sherry vinegar
½ cup olive oil
½ teaspoon coarsely crushed green or black peppercorns
1 teaspoon chopped fresh rosemary leaves

Whisk mustard, sugar and vinegar in a small bowl; gradually add oil, whisking until smooth. Whisk in peppercorns and rosemary. *Makes about ⅔ cup.*

the curious epicurean

Do you flambé or filet? Dice, mince or chop? Food terms can puzzle even the most experienced foodie. That's why we've taken the top terms and dissected them for you. So now you can get back to more important things. *Like eating.*

Chop:
To cut food into bite-size (or smaller) pieces. A food processor may also be used to chop food. Chopped food is larger in size than minced food.

Dice:
To cut food into small (about ⅛ inch to ¼ inch) cubes. Diced food is smaller in size than chopped food but larger than minced food.

Mince:
To cut food into very tiny pieces. Minced food is smaller in size than either chopped or diced food.

Water Bath:
The French call this cooking technique *bain marie*. It consists of placing a container of food in a shallow pan of warm water, allowing it to be cooked slowly and evenly.

Devein:
To remove the gray–black vein from the back of a shrimp. This can be done with the tip of a sharp knife or with a special tool called a deveiner.

Zest:
To remove the outermost skin layer of citrus fruit. Only the colored portion of the skin *(and not the white pith)* is considered the zest.

Flambé:
French for "flamed" or "flaming," this method of food presentation consists of sprinkling the food with liquor, slightly warming it, then igniting it just before serving.

Butterfly:
To split a food down the center, cutting almost but not completely through. The two halves are then opened flat to resemble a butterfly shape.

Julienne:
To cut food into very thin, matchstick-shaped strips. First cut food into ¼-inch-thick slices, stack, then cut into ¼-inch-thick strips. Finally, cut to desired length.

Blanch:
To plunge food (usually vegetables and fruits) briefly into boiling water, then immediately into cold water to stop the cooking process and retain its bright color.

Deglaze:
To heat a small amount of liquid in a pan where food has been sautéed in order to loosen the brown bits that have been left behind.

French:
To cut or trim the meat away from the end of a rib or a chop in order to expose a portion of the bone.

15

one sip soups

These one-shot wonders of bright, flavorful soup will have your guests reaching for seconds and thirds.

orange-scented carrot soup

¾ cup chopped onion

3 cloves garlic, crushed

2 tablespoons unsalted butter

1 tablespoon flour

1½ pounds carrots, sliced

2 cups chicken broth

½ teaspoon powdered ginger

¼ teaspoon ground cinnamon

1½-2 cups orange juice

Salt and white pepper, to taste

Julienne cucumbers, as garnish

Sauté onion and garlic in butter in large saucepan until onion is tender, about 5 minutes; stir in flour and cook 1 minute longer. Add carrots, chicken broth, ginger and cinnamon and bring to boil. Reduce heat and simmer, covered, until carrots are tender, about 15 minutes. Process soup mixture and 1½ cups orange juice in blender or food processor until smooth; stir in additional orange juice, if desired, for consistency. Season to taste with salt and white pepper. Serve appetizer portions in shot glasses or demitasse cups, or larger portions in mugs or small bowls; garnish with julienne cucumbers. *Makes 24 appetizer servings or 12 first-course servings.*

poblano chili soup

12 ounces poblano chilies, seeded, chopped (3 cups)

1½ cups chopped onions

3 cloves garlic, crushed

2 tablespoons unsalted butter

1 tablespoon flour

4 cups chicken broth

½-¾ teaspoon ground cumin

Salt, to taste

Julienne radishes, as garnish

Sauté chilies, onions and garlic in butter in large saucepan until tender, about 8 minutes; stir in flour and cook 1 minute longer. Add chicken broth and cumin and bring to boil; reduce heat and simmer, covered, 10 minutes. Process soup mixture in blender or food processor until smooth; season to taste with salt. Serve appetizer portions in shot glasses or demitasse cups, or larger portions in mugs or small bowls; garnish with julienne radishes. *Makes 24 appetizer servings or 12 first-course servings.*

roasted red pepper soup

⅔ cup chopped onion
2 cloves garlic, crushed
2 tablespoons unsalted butter
1 tablespoon flour
1 jar (24 ounces) roasted red bell peppers, undrained
1 can (14½ ounces) diced tomatoes, undrained
¼ cup sliced sun-dried tomatoes (not in oil)
1 cup chicken broth
½ teaspoon dried basil leaves
½ teaspoon dried thyme leaves
½ cup sour cream
Salt and pepper, to taste
Julienne beets, as garnish

Sauté onion and garlic in butter in large saucepan until tender, about 5 minutes; stir in flour and cook 1 minute longer. Add roasted peppers, tomatoes and juice, sun-dried tomatoes, chicken broth and herbs and bring to boil. Reduce heat and simmer, covered, 10 minutes. Process soup mixture in blender or food processor until smooth; stir in sour cream. Season to taste with salt and pepper. Serve appetizer portions in shot glasses or demitasse cups, or larger portions in mugs or small bowls; garnish with julienne beets. *Makes 24 appetizer servings or 12 first-course servings.*

dilled beet soup

⅔ cup chopped onion
2 tablespoons unsalted butter
1 tablespoon flour
1½ pounds beets, peeled, cut into 1-inch pieces
2½ cups chicken broth
1-2 tablespoons red wine vinegar
½-¾ teaspoon dried dill weed
½ cup sour cream
Salt and pepper, to taste
Julienne carrots, as garnish

Sauté onion in butter in large saucepan until tender, about 5 minutes; add flour and cook 1 minute longer. Add beets, chicken broth, vinegar and dill and bring to boil; reduce heat and simmer, covered, until beets are tender, 10 to 15 minutes. Process soup mixture in blender or food processor until smooth; stir in sour cream. Season to taste with salt and pepper. Serve small portions in shot glasses or demitasse cups, or larger portions in mugs or small bowls; garnish with julienne carrots. *Makes 24 appetizer servings or 12 first-course servings.*

Cook's Tip: All soups can be made and refrigerated 3 to 4 days in advance, or frozen up to 3 months.

festive feta and avocado salsa

Recipe inspired by Karen Kriaris

A "perfect for a party" salsa, with chunky bits of tomato, avocado and feta.

2-3 tablespoons olive oil
2 tablespoons lemon juice
2 cloves garlic, minced
¼ cup finely chopped parsley
1½ teaspoons dried oregano leaves
⅛ teaspoon red pepper flakes
1 cup cubed avocado
1 cup chopped tomatoes
¼ cup chopped red onion
½ cup (2 ounces) cubed feta cheese
Salt and pepper, to taste
Assorted tortilla chips, for dipping

Mix olive oil, lemon juice, garlic, parsley, oregano and pepper flakes in small bowl; set aside. Combine avocado, tomatoes and red onion in separate bowl; add olive oil mixture and toss. Add feta cheese and toss gently. Season to taste with salt and pepper. Serve in martini glasses or in a serving bowl with tortilla chips. *Makes 4 servings.*

wasabi reds

A sour cream-and-wasabi-laced filling gives tiny red potatoes big flavor.

24 tiny red potatoes (about 1-inch diameter), boiled 6-8 minutes, chilled
3 tablespoons melted butter
Salt and pepper, to taste
½ cup sour cream
½ teaspoon wasabi paste
1 tablespoon each black, golden and red lumpfish caviar
Chive strips, as garnish

Using a melon baller, scoop a small amount from the center of each potato. Place potatoes on cookie sheet; brush lightly with butter and sprinkle with salt and pepper. Broil 6 inches from heat source until lightly browned, 3 to 4 minutes. Cool. Mix together sour cream and wasabi paste. Spoon 1 teaspoon sour cream mixture into center of each potato; top with ⅛ teaspoon of each kind of caviar and garnish with chives. *Makes 12 servings.*

note.

Hot for Wasabi

It's spicy. It's green. And you've probably seen it as both a powder and a paste. So what exactly is wasabi? Quite simply, it's the Japanese version of horseradish. And it's known for giving foods a little fiery kick. If you've ever wondered what the difference is between its paste and powdered form, the answer is not much. In either case, the flavor is the same, so it really just boils down to what you like best—the ease of a paste in a tube or the flexibility of mixing a bit of water with the powder to form a paste.

"

TO *dish,*
or not TO DISH,
THAT *is*
the QUESTION.

"

sweet on swedish pancakes

These slightly sweet (and entirely fabulous) pancakes have a pear-and-cheese filling that will leave your guests swooning.

2 medium pears, ripe, but firm

2 tablespoons unsalted butter

⅓ cup sugar

1 tablespoon finely chopped fresh rosemary

Swedish Pancakes (recipe follows), warm

3 ounces Havarti cheese, cut into thin slices

Rosemary sprigs, as garnish

Peel and core pears, then cut into ½-inch slices, leaving stems attached to some. Melt butter in large skillet and add pears; sprinkle with combined sugar and rosemary and toss. Cook over medium-high heat, stirring occasionally, until pears are tender and lightly browned, about 5 minutes. Using tongs, place a pear slice on one side of a pancake; top with a slice of cheese and fold pancake in half. Repeat with remaining pears, pancakes and cheese. Arrange pancakes on serving platter; garnish with rosemary sprigs. *Makes 12 servings.*

swedish pancakes

2 eggs

¼ cup melted unsalted butter

2 teaspoons sugar

Pinch of salt

⅔ cup all-purpose flour

1¼ cups milk

In a large bowl, beat eggs, butter, sugar and salt until smooth. Whisk in flour until smooth; gradually whisk in milk (batter will be thin). Heat large, greased skillet over medium heat. Spoon batter into skillet, using 1 tablespoon for each pancake. Cook until browned, 2 to 3 minutes on each side. Remove from skillet and keep warm, loosely covered, in 200-degree oven. *Makes 2 dozen.*

Cook's Tip: Cooled pancakes can be stacked between layers of waxed paper and refrigerated up to 2 days or frozen up to 2 months. To reheat, place chilled or thawed pancakes on cookie sheet and bake at 300 degrees, covered with aluminum foil, until warm, 5 to 10 minutes.

herbed goat cheese balls

Fun combinations of herbs and spices pretty up bite-sized bits of goat cheese.

1 pound plain or herbed goat cheese, room temperature

Garnishes: your choice of any fresh herbs, spices, seeds or nuts

Pictured at right:

Black sesame seeds

Fresh thyme leaves

Finely chopped pistachio nuts with grated orange zest

Additional suggested garnishes:

Paprika

Chopped fresh rosemary

Finely chopped almonds, toasted

Finely chopped, candied ginger with chopped dried apricot

Roll goat cheese into balls, using 1 tablespoon for each. Transfer to baking sheet; refrigerate for 10 minutes to slightly set. Place desired garnishes into separate bowls. Roll balls in garnishes until coated. *Makes 16 servings.*

Cook's Tip: To make stripes, sprinkle chosen garnish in a thin straight line onto a cutting board and roll cheese ball down line.

from focaccia with love

Recipe inspired by Judith Mihalic

You'll fall head over heels for this yummy focaccia dotted with Vidalias, blue cheese and sun-dried tomatoes.

Focaccia Dough (recipe follows)

4 cups sliced Vidalia onions

2 teaspoons minced garlic

1 teaspoon dried basil leaves

1 teaspoon dried rosemary leaves

⅓-½ cup olive oil

1 cup (4 ounces) crumbled blue cheese

⅓ cup sliced sun-dried tomatoes (not in oil)

Make Focaccia Dough and let rise; punch dough down. Spread dough in greased 13x9-inch baking pan. Sauté onions, garlic and herbs in olive oil in large skillet, 3 to 4 minutes; cover and cook over medium heat until very tender, 8 to 10 minutes. Uncover and cook until beginning to brown, 2 to 3 minutes. Make indentations in dough with fingers; spread onion mixture evenly over dough. Sprinkle with blue cheese and sun-dried tomatoes. Bake at 375 degrees until crust is lightly browned, about 20 minutes. Cut into wedges or squares to serve. *Makes 16 servings.*

focaccia dough

3-3½ cups all-purpose flour, divided

1 package quick-rising yeast

1¼ cups hot water (120-130 degrees)

2 tablespoons olive oil

¼ teaspoon dried basil leaves

¼ teaspoon dried rosemary leaves

1 teaspoon salt

focaccia dough (cont'd)

Combine 1 cup flour and the yeast in large bowl; add water, stirring until smooth. Stir in olive oil, basil, rosemary and salt. Add enough remaining flour to make a soft dough. Knead dough on floured surface until smooth and elastic, about 5 minutes. Let dough rise in covered bowl 30 minutes.

Cook's Tip: Focaccia Dough can also be shaped into an 11-inch round on greased 12-inch pizza pan or into two 7-inch rounds on greased cookie sheets. Complete as above.

note.

A Brief History of Mini-Bites: Hors d'oeuvres

The French phrase "hors d'oeuvres" literally means "outside the works." And originally it wasn't a food term at all but actually an architectural term, referring to a building not incorporated into the architect's main design. So how did it come to be associated with food? Well, French culinary experts eventually borrowed it, using it to designate the small dishes served "outside of" the main course of a dinner.

savory smoked salmon cheesecake

Recipe inspired by Deborah Egizii

Smoked salmon takes cheesecake from the sweet to the savory—not to mention the "sooo delicious."

⅔ cup chopped roasted red pepper

½ cup finely chopped onion

2 cloves garlic, minced

1 tablespoon olive oil

2 8-oz packages cream cheese, softened

3 eggs

½ cup grated Parmesan cheese

1 teaspoon Worcestershire sauce

3-4 drops hot pepper sauce

2 tablespoons flour

½ teaspoon salt

6 ounces nova lox or smoked fresh salmon, finely chopped

½ cup chopped green onions and tops

Buttery Cracker-Pecan Crust (recipe follows)

Baby greens, as garnish

Pumpernickel cocktail bread or melba toast

To make a whole cheesecake: Sauté roasted red pepper, onion and garlic in oil in medium skillet until onion is tender, 3 to 4 minutes; cool. Beat cream cheese in large bowl until fluffy; beat in eggs. Beat in Parmesan cheese, Worcestershire sauce, hot pepper sauce, flour and salt. Mix in cooled onion mixture, smoked salmon and green onions; pour into Buttery Cracker-Pecan Crust. Wrap bottom and side of pan with heavy-duty aluminum foil and place in roasting pan on middle oven rack. Add 1 inch hot water to roasting pan. Bake at 325 degrees until cheesecake is set but slightly soft in the center, 40 to 50 minutes. Cool on wire rack. Refrigerate, covered, 8 hours or overnight. Remove side of pan and transfer cheesecake to serving plate. Garnish with baby greens; serve with bread and melba toast. *Makes 24 servings.*

buttery cracker-pecan crust

1 cup ground butter-flavor club crackers

½ cup finely chopped pecans

4 tablespoons butter, melted

Combine all ingredients in bottom of 8- or 9-inch springform pan; press mixture evenly on bottom and 1 inch up side of pan. Bake at 350 degrees until lightly browned, 6 to 8 minutes. Cool. *Makes one 8- or 9-inch crust.*

Variation: To make individual cheesecakes, triple the Buttery Cracker-Pecan Crust recipe. Pat ¼ cup crumb mixture in bottom and up sides of paper-lined or silicone muffin cup; repeat, making 18 cups. Make cheesecake filling and fill crusts, using scant ¼ cup mixture for each. Bake at 325 degrees until cheesecakes are just set, about 25 minutes. Cool and refrigerate overnight.

garnishes: food's favorite accessory

What better way to make your apps even more appetizing than by dressing them up with some inspired garnishes? From the simple to the *"now why didn't I think of that,"* we've listed our faves that'll add a little finesse to any finger food.

Micro Greens
PART 1

Micro greens are pretty much just the mini-versions of their grown-up counterparts (think arugula, basil or radish leaves, even). And because of their great color, intriguing size and robust flavor, they go a long way toward dressing up a dish.

Micro Greens
PART 2

Mix and match several varieties and use them as a bed under appetizers that tend to be more greasy. The greens will not only soak up the messy liquids but they'll also serve as a colorful—and creative—presentation idea.

Herbs

For a sassier take on skewers, go beyond bamboo and use herbs. Rosemary sprigs, lemon grass stalks and thyme branches are all great for skewering meats and fish.

Spices

Get heavy-handed with your spices: sprinkle a solid layer of a colorful spice (such as paprika) on a platter to create a bright and flavorful serving background.

Vegetables

Soak julienned vegetables such as carrots, cucumbers and peppers in ice water for a few minutes, watch them delicately curl, then use them as toppers and garnishes.

Fruits

For a twist on the traditional lemon zest garnish, use a knife to peel a lemon (or any citrus fruit, really) apple-style so that you end up with long, spiraling strips of peel. Use these to bundle asparagus spears or to tie around poached scallops.

Oils & Sauces

Use a plastic squeeze bottle filled with your favorite flavored oil or some reserved cooking sauce to draw decorative designs onto your serving platters.

Butter
PART 1

Butter made better: soften butter, place it in candy molds, then freeze until hardened. Once set, pop each mini butter pat out and serve (or keep refrigerated until ready to use).

Butter
PART 2

Give foods a tastier twist with compound butters: bring unsalted butter to room temp, then mix in your favorite herbs or spices (herbs should be finely chopped). Let stand for 2 hours to meld flavors. Keep refrigerated in an airtight container up to 1 month.

spinach pesto

Spinach takes center stage in this anything-but-traditional take on pesto.

3 cups lightly packed spinach leaves

⅓ cup olive oil

¼ cup pistachio nuts

¼ cup (1 ounce) shredded Romano cheese

3 tablespoons orange juice

1 clove garlic

2 tablespoons grated orange zest

2 tablespoons sliced sun-dried tomatoes (not in oil)

Salt and pepper, to taste

Sliced sun-dried tomatoes, as garnish

Melba toasts and thin bread sticks

Process spinach, olive oil, pistachio nuts, Romano cheese, orange juice, garlic and orange zest in food processor until smooth; add sun-dried tomatoes and process until coarsely chopped. Season to taste with salt and pepper. Spoon Spinach Pesto into bowl and garnish with sliced sun-dried tomatoes. Serve with melba toasts and bread sticks. *Makes 6 servings.*

Cook's Tip: Pesto can be made and refrigerated 3 to 4 days in advance; serve at room temperature.

shrimp-a-go-go

Recipe inspired by Donna Pranio

Get your party go-go-going with these delicious bacon-wrapped, grilled shrimp.

4 slices bacon, halved

8 Scallion Brushes (recipe follows)

8 extra large shrimp, peeled, deveined and butterflied

½ cup apricot preserves

1 teaspoon sherry vinegar or white wine vinegar

½ teaspoon sesame oil

¼ cup chopped peanuts

Cook bacon slices in simmering water in small saucepan, 3 minutes; drain on paper towels. Place a Scallion Brush in the center of each butterflied shrimp; wrap each with a piece of bacon and secure with a wooden toothpick. Cook shrimp over medium heat in a large skillet or broil 6 inches from heat source until bacon is crisp and shrimp are cooked, about 5 minutes, turning frequently. In separate bowl, mix apricot preserves, vinegar, sesame oil and peanuts; serve with shrimp. *Makes 4 servings.*

scallion brushes

8 thin scallions

Trim scallions to a length of 4 inches. Cut white end of each into thin strips with sharp knife or scissors. Place in ice water until ends curl.

Cause a stir.
Make your tiny nibblers that much more nosh-worthy by adding a few inventive embellishments to your drinks and glassware. *From Left to Right:* Garnish with a large yellow watermelon and lemon slice; wrap a banana leaf around a glass filled with thin cucumber shavings; place pretty red currants in small tumblers; clip a fun accoutrement (we used a little pinwheel) onto a glass's edge; freeze fresh berries in ice cube trays; dress up a drink with thin stalks of sugar cane and paper umbrellas.

"

Whip OUT
YOUR *best* MANNERS—
eat with your
FINGERS.

"

mesquite chicken and toasted pecan pâté

Smoky chicken, toasted pecans and a hint of mango give this luscious pâté pizzazz.

½ cup pecan halves or pieces

2 teaspoons unsalted butter

2 tablespoons sliced green onion tops

4 large parsley sprigs

4 ounces mesquite-smoked chicken breast, cut into ½-inch cubes

3 ounces white Cheddar cheese, shredded

¼ cup sour cream

2 tablespoons chopped mango chutney

Gourmet crackers, crusty bread, zucchini slices

Cook pecans in butter over medium heat in small skillet until browned, 3 to 4 minutes. Cool. Process pecans, green onions and parsley in food processor until finely chopped. Add chicken and cheese; process until finely chopped. Pour into bowl; mix in sour cream and chutney. Refrigerate, covered, 24 hours for flavors to blend. Fill lightly greased 1-ounce mini tart pans with pâté mixture and refrigerate until serving time; remove from pans and arrange on serving plate. Or, spoon pâté into a crock or mound on a plate. Serve with assorted crackers. *Makes 12 servings.*

Cook's Tip: To unmold tart pans easily, place in freezer for a few minutes until firm, then pop out of pans. Pâté can be made and refrigerated 3 to 4 days in advance or frozen up to 2 months.

note.

*Pâté
Unplugged*

Despite what many people think, pâté is much more than just chopped liver. French for "pie," pâté can actually be a mixture of a wide variety of seasoned ground meats, seafoods or vegetables. What's more, it's commonly prepared in crusts (en croûte) or molds, often called terrines.

roasted grape and mascarpone bruschetta

Recipe inspired by Amy Wiles

Sweet, roasted fruit and creamy mascarpone top this simple yet sophisticated bruschetta.

16 baguette slices (about ½ inch thick)
1 large garlic clove, halved
8 ounces mascarpone cheese, room temperature
2 tablespoons chopped, toasted walnuts
48 red seedless grapes, halved
Freshly ground pepper, to taste
1-2 tablespoons honey

Toast bread slices; lightly rub top of each slice with cut sides of garlic halves. Spread each bread slice with 1 tablespoon mascarpone cheese; sprinkle with walnuts and top each with 6 grape halves. Sprinkle with ground pepper and drizzle with honey. Broil, 4 inches from heat source, until warm, 1 to 2 minutes. *Makes 8 servings (2 each).*

Variation: Fresh or dried figs can be substituted for the grapes. Use one fresh fig halved or 2-3 dried figs per bruschetta.

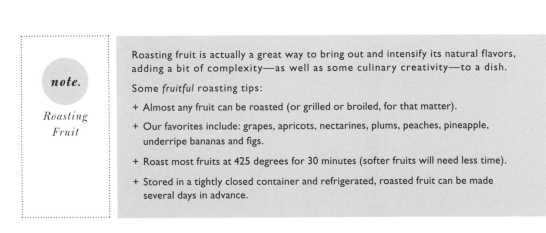

note.

Roasting Fruit

Roasting fruit is actually a great way to bring out and intensify its natural flavors, adding a bit of complexity—as well as some culinary creativity—to a dish.

Some *fruitful* roasting tips:

+ Almost any fruit can be roasted (or grilled or broiled, for that matter).

+ Our favorites include: grapes, apricots, nectarines, plums, peaches, pineapple, underripe bananas and figs.

+ Roast most fruits at 425 degrees for 30 minutes (softer fruits will need less time).

+ Stored in a tightly closed container and refrigerated, roasted fruit can be made several days in advance.

To: Lily,
Time to get tropical.
Saturday, 6 p.m.
See you lei-ter! —Tiff

make a scene with style

When it comes to a party, the scene you set is just as important as the snacks you serve. Get inspired with these creative ideas for themes, invites, decorations and more.

Inviting Invites:

+ Having a Cheese Party? Use a hole punch to randomly punch small holes into brightly colored orange craft paper to create a Swiss-cheese-inspired invite.

+ For something more tropical, attach leaf-shaped cards to pretty leis.

+ Lights! Camera! Party! Send out invitations for an awards-themed bash in fun film canisters.

+ If the beach is your muse, make invites by threading shells onto ribbon and adorning with a shell-shaped card.

Think Themes:

+ Pick a color, any color—decorate in one or two colors, carrying your theme through to even your food. Going green? Serve green-colored punches and soups, set out bowls of pistachios or edamame and include green veggies like asparagus and artichokes in your fare.

Bringing the Outdoors In:

+ A blooming good idea—wrap single stems of silk or fabric flowers around napkins for an inventive new look and fun burst of color.

+ Depending on the season, gather gourds or mini pumpkins into bowls as centerpieces. Fresh cherries (or any smaller fruit) mounded on a cake plate work equally well.

"

FOR *A*
CHEESE *called* BLUE,
IT SURE DOES
taste HAPPY.

"

sweet honey blues

Recipe inspired by Linda Chuderewicz

Sweet and sassy is how we describe these crackers topped with gooey, golden honey and rich Gorgonzola.

12 ounces Gorgonzola or other blue-veined cheese, chilled

24 gourmet crackers

1-2 ounces honeycomb, cut into 24 pieces

Walnut pieces, toasted

Cut cheese into 24 slices and place on crackers. Top each with one piece of honeycomb and sprinkle with walnuts. *Makes 12 servings.*

Cook's Tip: Regular honey without the comb can be substituted. Drizzle each cracker with ½ teaspoon honey and sprinkle with walnuts.

note.

So What Makes a Blue Cheese Blue?

As unsavory as it might sound, all those blue and blue-green squiggly lines in blue cheese (from Stilton to Gorgonzola to Roquefort and more) are mold. Legend has it that the discovery of blue cheese was actually an accident—the cheese, originally stored in caves for aging, developed mold and was thought to be ruined. That is, until one brave soul decided to have a taste and discovered just how delicious its flavor had become. As you might expect, most blue cheeses today are not created by "accident," but instead have the mold either injected or mixed right in with the curds. It is, however, still aged in the caves of the area that bears its name.

the perfect cheese tray: a slice-by-slice guide

From what kinds to buy to the perfect way to serve it, here are some basic guidelines to help make your next cheese tray *"très" fabulous.*

Buying:

For the most visually interesting and party-worthy platter, select 3-6 cheeses that vary in shape, color, texture and flavor. A good place to start is by choosing at least one cheese from each of the four basic categories: *Aged, Soft, Firm and Blue.*

Never forget the cardinal rule of cheese buying: Always taste before you buy. After all, it's the best way to determine if you'll truly enjoy a particular cheese. This is especially true if you find yourself venturing into uncharted cheese territory.

If all those cheese counter choices prove to be a conundrum, think themes—consider buying all blues or a sampling of different goat cheeses or even cheeses from the same region or by the same cheesemaker.

Serving:

Cheese is best when served at room temperature. That means, at least one hour before guests arrive, be sure to remove it from the refrigerator. And don't forget to leave cheese covered until just before serving, as this will prevent it from drying out.

Give your cheese some elbow room. Make sure your serving surface is large enough to fit all your cheeses comfortably, with enough space between each so your guests can cut them easily.

While the cheese is the hero, the sides you serve along with it are far from second fiddle. In fact, getting creative with accompaniments can actually help to enhance a cheese's flavor:

+ Crusty bread, fresh fruits (think pears, peaches or figs) and Medjool dates complement all cheese types.
+ Chutneys pair perfectly with Cheddar, especially aged varieties.
+ Olives, roasted peppers and tomatoes are a good match for fresh goat cheeses.

Think outside the tray—don't be shy about serving up your cheese on something other than the classic, rustic board. Bright, bold platters in fun shapes, earthy marbles and stone surfaces can all take your cheese tray from the expected to the exceptional.

Storing:

It's a wrap—the best material for storing cheese is parchment paper (it slows down oxidation while still allowing the cheese to breathe). If you don't have any handy, use cheesecloth, wax paper or even aluminum foil. What not to use? Plastic wrap—it blocks out air completely.

Cheeses Featured (clockwise from top, starting with pyramid): Valancey Aged Goat; Cow's Milk; Lingot du Quercy Aged Goat; (bottom wedge behind fruit) Parmigiano-Reggiano; (top wedge) Smoked Gouda; (center, top round) Le Chevrot; (bottom round) Selles sur Cher.

red pepper relish

Cheese meets its match when served alongside this tart and tangy relish-with-a-kick.

1½ cups thinly sliced red bell peppers

1½ cups thinly sliced red onions

1-2 teaspoons minced jalapeño

3 tablespoons olive oil

¼ cup packed light brown sugar

¼ cup cider vinegar

¼ cup water

Assorted cheeses (Brie, Cheddar, asiago), room temperature

Sauté bell peppers, onions and jalapeño in oil in large skillet until softened, about 5 minutes. Stir in brown sugar, vinegar and water and simmer, covered, over medium-low heat until very tender, about 10 minutes. Uncover and simmer rapidly until mixture is glazed and thickened, 3 to 4 minutes; cool. Serve at room temperature with cheeses. *Makes 6 servings.*

Cook's Tip: Red Pepper Relish can be made and refrigerated, covered, 4 to 5 days in advance. Serve at room temperature.

garlic shrimp with cheddar grits

You don't have to be Southern to fall for this tasty bite-sized version of the classic shrimp and grits.

Cheddar Grits (recipe follows)
1 pound medium shrimp, peeled, deveined
1-2 teaspoons minced garlic
6 tablespoons unsalted butter, divided
2 tablespoons lemon juice
Salt and pepper, to taste

Make Cheddar Grits and keep warm. Sauté shrimp and garlic in 3 tablespoons butter in large skillet until shrimp are almost cooked and pink, 3 to 4 minutes. Add lemon juice and cook until shrimp are beginning to brown and skillet is almost dry, 2 to 3 minutes; add remaining 3 tablespoons butter to skillet and remove from heat. Season to taste with salt and pepper. Spoon Cheddar Grits onto appetizer spoons or small plates; top with shrimp and drizzle with remaining butter in skillet. *Makes 12 appetizer servings or 4 first-course servings.*

cheddar grits

½ teaspoon minced garlic
1 tablespoon unsalted butter
2 cups water
½ teaspoon salt
½ cup yellow grits
½ cup (2 ounces) grated Cheddar cheese

Sauté garlic in butter in medium saucepan until tender, about 1 minute; add water and salt, bring to boil. Gradually stir in grits; cook according to time indicated on package. Add cheese and stir until melted; serve warm. *Makes about 2 cups.*

Cook's Tip: Grits can be made and refrigerated 2 to 3 days in advance. Reheat in saucepan over medium heat until warm, stirring frequently.

cranberry-pistachio brie

Recipe inspired by Pat Swihart

Warm, creamy Brie gets all dressed up with cranberry and pistachios.

½ small onion, thinly sliced
1 tablespoon unsalted butter
⅓ cup dried cranberries
¼ cup orange juice
⅓ cup coarsely chopped shelled pistachio nuts
¼ cup apricot preserves
1 wheel (13½ ounces) Brie cheese
Crusty bread and assorted crackers

Sauté onion in butter in medium skillet until tender, 3 to 4 minutes. Add cranberries and orange juice; bring to boil. Reduce heat and simmer until orange juice is absorbed, about 5 minutes. Stir in pistachios and preserves. Remove rind from top of cheese with sharp knife. Place cheese on microwave-safe serving plate; spread cranberry mixture on cheese and refrigerate. At serving time, microwave on high power until cheese is just softened, 30 to 45 seconds. Serve with crusty bread and assorted crackers.

Makes 8 to 10 servings.

Cook's Tip: Brie can be assembled and refrigerated 2 to 3 hours in advance; microwave as above before serving.

"

Salt.
It's THE
little BLACK *dress*
of COOKING.

"

scallop bundles with orange-tarragon butter

Expect to be bowled over by these gift-wrapped bundles of tender, orange-scented scallops.

1 leek, green top only
1 large carrot, halved lengthwise
16-18 sea scallops (1¼ pounds)
1 cup orange juice
Grated rind of 1 orange
2 teaspoons finely chopped green onion
1 dried bay leaf
Orange-Tarragon Butter Sauce (recipe follows)

Cut leek top into 16 to 18 strips, 6 inches long and ¼ inch wide. Make 16 to 18 long strips of carrot with vegetable peeler. Blanch leeks and carrots in simmering water until limp, 1 to 2 minutes; drain on paper towels. Wrap a carrot strip around a scallop and tie with a leek; repeat with remaining scallops, carrots and leeks. Bring orange juice, orange rind, green onion and bay leaf to a boil in medium skillet. Arrange scallops in skillet in single layer; reduce heat and simmer, covered, until scallops are cooked, 4 to 5 minutes. Remove scallops and keep warm; strain broth, reserving 1 cup. Make Orange-Tarragon Butter Sauce. Arrange scallops in shell dishes or rimmed serving dish; spoon Orange-Tarragon Butter Sauce over. *Makes 8 appetizer servings or 6 first-course servings.*

orange-tarragon butter sauce

4 tablespoons unsalted butter
2 tablespoons flour
1 cup reserved cooking broth from scallops
2 teaspoons lemon juice
¼ teaspoon dried tarragon leaves
Salt and cayenne pepper, to taste

Melt butter in small saucepan; add flour and cook, stirring, 1 to 2 minutes. Gradually whisk in reserved broth, lemon juice and tarragon; bring to boil, whisking until slightly thickened, about 1 minute. Season to taste with salt and cayenne pepper. *Makes 1¼ cups.*

a sandwich soirée

Mini sandwiches get all grown up in this trio of savory snacks.

petite pork tenderloin burgers

½ cup thinly sliced red onion
¼ cup red wine vinegar
1 teaspoon chopped garlic
1 tablespoon curry powder
1 teaspoon each, salt and pepper
¼ cup lemon juice
12 ounces pork tenderloin, cut into 12 slices
⅔ cup coarsely ground cashews or almonds
1 tablespoon unsalted butter
1 tablespoon canola oil
12 small sandwich rolls, split
¾ cup mango chutney

Combine red onion and vinegar in small bowl; let stand 1 hour. Drain. Combine garlic,
curry powder, salt and pepper on cutting board and mash with side of knife to make a
smooth paste; combine with lemon juice in small bowl. Pound pork slices between pieces of
waxed paper until ⅛ inch thick. Brush pork slices with lemon mixture and coat generously
with cashews. Heat half the butter and oil in large skillet over medium-low heat; add half
the pork slices and cook until no longer pink in the center, 2 to 3 minutes on each side.
Remove from skillet and keep warm. Wipe out skillet; heat remaining butter and oil and
cook remaining pork slices. Place pork slices in buns, topping each slice with red onion
and a tablespoon of chutney. *Makes 12 servings.*

chicken gouda pumpernickel squares

1 cup finely chopped cooked chicken breast
¼ cup finely chopped celery
¼ cup (1 ounce) shredded smoked Gouda
2 tablespoons finely chopped onion
2 tablespoons coarsely chopped dried cherries
2 tablespoons chopped toasted almonds
½ cup mayonnaise
Salt and pepper, to taste
24 slices cocktail pumpernickel bread
Assorted baby greens, as garnish

Mix together first seven ingredients; season to taste with salt and pepper. Spoon
1 tablespoon chicken mixture onto each bread slice; garnish with assorted baby greens.
Makes 12 servings.
Cook's Tip: Chicken mixture can be made and refrigerated 1 day in advance.

mini gyros burgers with feta aioli

12 ounces ground lamb
12 ounces ground beef
¼ cup finely chopped parsley
3 tablespoons finely chopped onion
3 tablespoons finely chopped roasted red bell pepper
2 teaspoons chopped garlic
1 tablespoon chopped fresh or 1 teaspoon dried oregano leaves
1 teaspoon salt
¼ teaspoon pepper
24 thin cucumber slices
12 mini pita breads or small sandwich rolls
Feta Aioli (recipe follows)
Mixed baby greens, as garnish

Mix together first nine ingredients; shape into 12 two-inch patties. Cook patties in large skillet over medium heat to desired doneness, 2 to 3 minutes on each side for medium. Place burgers and cucumber slices in pita breads; spoon 1 tablespoon Feta Aioli into each pita. Garnish with baby greens. *Makes 12 servings.*

feta aioli

1 teaspoon chopped garlic
⅛ teaspoon salt
½ cup mayonnaise
⅓ cup crumbled feta cheese
2 tablespoons chopped roasted red pepper

Combine garlic and salt on cutting board, mash with side of knife to make smooth paste; combine with remaining ingredients in small bowl. *Makes about ¾ cup.*

Cook's Tip: Aioli can be made and refrigerated up to 2 days in advance.

parsley, sage, rosemary and galangal

From the far-out (f.y.i.—galangal is an Indian root similar to ginger) to the far more familiar (who hasn't heard of parsley?), herbs and spices, along with the aromas they impart, play a key role in how a dish tastes. Which is why knowing what's what in that spice rack of yours is pretty key, too. So enjoy this helpful guide. It not only gives you the *what's-what* but also the *what's-interesting* about your favorite flavorings.

Thyme:
Egyptians embalmed with it, Greeks bathed in it and during the Renaissance it was used as perfume. Today, thyme, with its peppery-flavored dark green leaves, is most often added to dishes to give them a unique depth.

Mint:
There are over 500 different types of mint (an herb once believed to spur one's appetite for meat). Enjoy its mild scent and fragrant flavor in both sweet and savory dishes, and be sure to look for leaves that are bright green with no bruising.

Garlic:
Its nickname is the "stinking rose," and whether powdered or fresh, it's known for giving foods a distinctive flavor. Pick heads that are firm to the touch, and remember this: the smaller you chop garlic, the more pungent it becomes.

Rosemary:
Hundreds of years ago, rosemary was dipped in gold, tied with ribbon and given as a keepsake at weddings. Whether fresh or dried, it's best to crush this herb in your hand or with a mortar and pestle before using to release its flavor.

Bay Leaf:
As a symbol of honor and celebration, the champions of the first Olympic games in 776 B.C. were crowned with garlands of this glossy, green leaf. Use it to add complexity to soups and stews, but always remember to remove before serving.

Basil:
In Romania, lads used to accept sprigs of basil from young maidens to signify their engagement. It's one of the easiest herbs to grow and one of the most versatile to cook with, giving validity to its name, which means "king."

Cinnamon:
It's one of the world's oldest seasonings and is actually stripped evergreen bark (who knew?). And while you might think it's synonymous with desserts, it's also great when used to flavor savory and meat dishes, as often done in the East.

Cumin:
Today it's the dominant flavoring in Latin American cooking, but long ago, the Romans and Greeks used it as a preservative. This pale-brown seed is actually a member of the parsley family and is known for its earthy, musty flavor.

Dill:
Back in ancient times, dill was considered a sign of wealth and was often burned in order to flaunt one's social status. It's most flavorful when fresh and tends to lose its intensity in heat, so only add it to hot dishes right before serving.

parmesan lace

Use your hands to curl these pretty lace crisps while they're still warm from the oven.

1 cup (4 ounces) finely shredded Parmesan cheese
1 teaspoon coarsely crushed mixed peppercorns (red, green, black)
¼ teaspoon dried thyme leaves
¼ teaspoon crumbled dried rosemary leaves
Mixed baby greens, as garnish

Toss cheese, peppercorns and herbs in bowl. Spoon tablespoons of cheese mixture, 3 inches apart, onto parchment-lined cookie sheet; spread gently with fingers into 3-inch rounds. Bake at 350 degrees until browned, 5 to 7 minutes. While cheese wafers are still warm and pliable, remove from pan and shape as desired with hands. Top or fill with baby greens.
Makes 16 large or 32 small wafers.

Cook's Tip: If making smaller wafers, spoon cheese mixture by ½ tablespoons, 3 inches apart, onto parchment-lined cookie sheet; spread into 2-inch rounds and bake as above. Parmesan Lace can be made up to 5 days in advance and stored at room temperature in an airtight container or frozen, layered between waxed paper, in an airtight container up to 2 months. Fill with baby greens before serving.

Light the way.
What better way to make your party really shine than with candles?
A little creativity and imagination can go a long way in adding a
little more *glow* to your gathering.

notes

notes

notes